Flying Tankers

Flying Tankers

— GAS STATIONS IN THE SKY —

Tim Laming

Published in 1989 by Osprey Publishing Limited
59 Grosvenor Street, London W1X 9DA

British Library Cataloguing in Publication Data

Laming, Tim
    Flying tankers: gas stations in the sky
    1. Military aircraft
    I. Title
    623. 74' 6

ISBN 0-85045-912-5

Editor Dennis Baldry
Designed by Paul Kime
Printed in Hong Kong

Front cover Thanks to the efforts of Sir Alan
Cobham, Britain established a world lead in flight
refuelling. On 22 September 1934 he departed from
Portsmouth for Karachi in the prototype Airspeed
AS 5 Courier. A successful refuelling rendezvous
took place over the Isle of Wight, with Cobham
snatching the trailing hose from a Handley Page
W10 through a hatch in the Courier's cabin. A
detailed account of Sir Alan Cobham's achievements
and those of his company, Flight Refuelling, are
beyond the scope of this modest volume, but his
leading role in getting the USAF into the flight
refuelling business must be mentioned. On 26
February 1949 a Boeing B-50 named *Lucky Lady II*,
took off from Fort Worth, Texas and flew a round
trip of 23,452 miles in 94 hours, ten minutes—the
first non-stop round the world flight. This epic
journey was made possible by Cobham's flight
refuelling equipment, which was installed in several
other B-50s positioned along the route. Today, the
RAF's VC-10 tankers are equipped with Flight
Refuelling FR.20B pods, seen here slaking the thirst
of two Lightning T.5s, from No 11 Sqn (grey
aircraft) and the Lightning Training Flight. Since this
picture was taken in 1987, the Lightning has been
retired from RAF service. No 11 Sqn is now
equipped with the Tornado F.3

Back cover An RAF Lockheed Hercules C.1K
tanker trails its hose for the benefit of a Hercules
C.1P receiver over the Atlantic. A similar picture is
featured inside

Title pages Boeing KC-135R of the 319th Bomb
Wing/905th Air Refueling Squadron, pictured at
RAF Fairford in 1988

Right A multi-aircraft rendezvous over the Atlantic
in March 1988, involving a No 216 Sqn TriStar,
two Buccaneers from No 12 Sqn, two Sea Harriers
from No 800 NAS, a VC10 K.3 from No 101 Sqn,
and a VC10 C.1 from No 10 Sqn

The world of air-to-air refuelling (AAR) doesn't receive much publicity. Tanker aircraft aren't exactly glamorous, but they play a vital part in the armoury of almost every major air arm. However, whilst the flying gas stations might be lacking in aesthetic beauty, their activities are fascinating in the extreme, so let's take a look at the world of AAR . . .

As a civilian in the world of military aviation, I must continually rely on the support of many individuals, who allow me access to machines and places that are normally reserved exclusively for military men and women. It would, of course, be impossible to thank every individual who assisted me with this book, but I must extend my sincere thanks to the following people in particular:

Jeff Halik and the Public Affairs staff at RAF Mildenhall, Keith Haywood and No 55 Sqn at RAF Marham, Mike Looseley, Simon Smith and No 208 Sqn, Terry Locke and the Tanker Training Flight at RAF Lyneham, Mark Ims (formerly of No 5(F) Sqn), Charlie Cantan and the crews of Nos 899 and 800 Naval Air Squadrons at Yeovilton, the members of No 19 Sqn at Wildenrath. Also my special thanks to Michael Hill, CPRO Strike Command.

Finally, my thanks to my fellow photographers who have assisted me in supplying some unique shots that I couldn't quite get myself! Air Portraits, Mike Jenvey, René J Francillon, Peter B Lewis, Fritz Becker and Ian and Stuart Black.

All the photographs in this volume were taken by the author except where credited, and were taken on Kodachrome KR64 film, using Canon T70 and T90 cameras, fitted with 18 mm, 35–70 mm, 200 mm and 300 mm lenses.

Heading for Scapa Flow, a Buccaneer S.2B from No 208 Sqn trails a buddy-pack refuelling hose

Contents

Stratotanker

Crew Chief prepares to remove his RT cable, as 60-0322 prepares to roll from the hardstanding on a cold morning at RAF Mildenhall in Suffolk, England

Right KC-135 derivatives might be the most common visitors to Mildenhall, but the KC-10 Extender is by far the biggest tanker around, and it too makes regular calls at 'The Hall', usually flying to or from the States

Above All of the UK-based KC-135 tankers are stationed on a TDY (Temporary Duty) detachment basis, for rotational periods lasting between four and seven weeks. The transient nature of Mildenhall's tanker crews is reflected by the ever-growing collection of unit 'zaps' which adorn the snack machines

Ready to close the entry hatch, the last member of the ground crew jumps down the ladder, while the Crew Chief checks the flying control surfaces for correct and effective functions

Left It takes a long time to settle into a KC-135, and to get all the systems up and working. The first job is to get all the luggage on board, and there's always lots of it. The last item looks like being the in-flight refreshments

Above What could be more frustrating? After having assembled before dawn, attended the briefings, planned the route, pre-flighted the aircraft, and prepared to start the engines, the receivers cancel, because the weather has clamped down over their airfield. So it's back to the Operations Building, after dumping the 670 US gals of take-off-boosting water

Left The CFM International F108-CF-100 turbofan is better known to you and me as the CFM56. It has revolutionized KC-135 operations, thanks to its lower fuel consumption and higher thrust (22,000 lb each). No more lumbering struggles down the runway; the KC-135R departs like a rocket

Above The Boeing-designed 'flying boom' is the standard USAF method of moving fuel from one aeroplane to another, in the air. Unlike the RAF (which fits the refuelling probe to the receiver), the tanker crew plug into the receiver's receptacle. Most KC-135s now have floodlights fitted to a fin-top extension

Overleaf 29,000 feet over the West German Navy air base at Nordholz, the crew of 60-0322 are getting close to the East/West 'buffer zone', where their customers will be waiting; three RF-4C Phantom IIs

17

Left One of the latest 'mods' to the flight deck is a digital fuel control panel. The main bank of dials relates to oil pressure (bottom), fuel flow, engine inner core RPM, and outer fan RPM (top)

Above Behind the pilot and copilot, Tony Rocco is navigating, and making sure that we don't stray from our intended course even by an inch. We're a little too close to the 'buffer zone' to risk getting lost! 'Oh there's no problem with Tony—he's a wizard with the radar. He worked with Marconi'

Top left Behind the flight deck, the huge, darkened fuselage provides ample space for cargo and personnel (up to 160 troops). Plenty of room for the Boom Operator to check his fuel transfer loads, too

Left Keep walking down the fuselage, and right at the end you'll find the entry hatch into the Boom Operator's position. Over on the right-hand side is the Auxiliary Power Unit—another of the KC-135R's retrofits

Above There are three couches: one for the Boom Operator, one for an instructor and/or observer as required. Lying face down, there's a great view to be had, looking out under the rear fuselage

Above The 'Boomer' spends most of his (or her) career peering out through the rear window. At heights of 25,000 feet or more, it's often quite cold. A cup of hot coffee helps

Right The 'Boomer's' control panel features the joystick for 'flying' the refuelling boom into position. The various external lighting modes are controlled here too, including the Pilot Director Lights (PDLs), which indicate to the receiver pilot his relative height to the tanker

From the outside, the PDL strips can be seen under
the forward fuselage of this KC-135Q (*Courtesy René
J Francillon*)

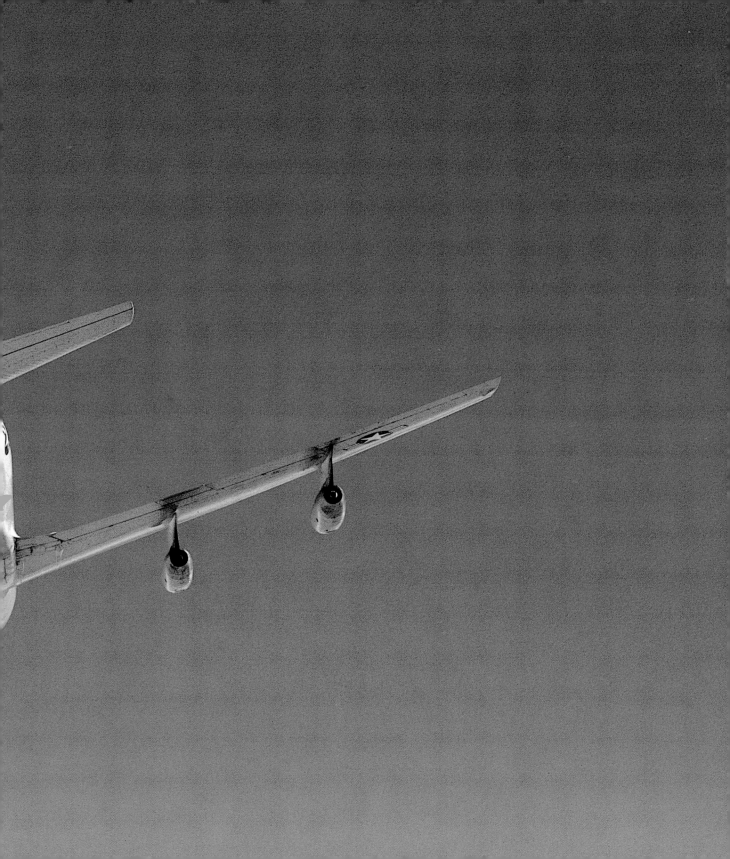

Our first customer, an RF-4C Phantom II from the
26th Tactical Reconnaissance Wing, on a mission
from its home base at Zweibrucken. The receptacle
is open and fuel is streaming down the fuselage

Left Call sign XEROX ONE (pretty appropriate for a photo-recce aircraft), the oblique sunlight shows the patchy 'European One' camouflage and the rough surface on the non-slip walkways

Above Good morning, Major Ginrich. Getting intimate with the Phantom's cockpit as the Weapon Systems Officer (WSO) in back checks that the plugged-in probe doesn't come any closer

Full of juice, XEROX ONE heads off to depart to
low level. Have a nice day!

Above No prizes for spotting that this KC-135 is an 'R' model. The big 'trash cans' under the wings make an aircraft spotter's life too easy. Gear and flaps are down as the aircraft tracks the approach lights

Right Major Al Andersen guides a KC-135R of the 384th Air Refuelling Sqn, Heavy, onto a refuelling track over Northern Germany during a mission from RAF Fairford on 12 October 1988. In addition to her crew, LAGER 62 also had photographers David Davies and Mike Vines of Air Portraits on board as well as Osprey's Aerospace Editor, Dennis Baldry (*Courtesy Air Portraits*)

Top left An Upper Heyford-based EF-111A Raven electronic warfare aircraft, call sign VOLT 13(!) approaches LAGER 62 for a drink of JP-4 (*Courtesy Air Portraits*)

Left Stateside: this quartet of KC-135A Stratotankers are part of a 43-strong fleet belonging to the 924th Air Refueling Squadron/93rd Bomb Wing, at Castle AFB in California (*Courtesy René J Francillon*)

Above A quartet of Lakenheath's F-111F strike aircraft demonstrate a tight rendezvous formation behind one of Mildenhall's tankers. Standard procedure is for the receivers to formate off the starboard wing prior to positioning for refuelling, and then to move out to the port side, prior to departure

Above Big tankers need big hangars. The business end is safely sheltered, but the tail has to stay *al fresco* (*Courtesy Peter B Lewis*)

Right The KC-135Q crews might be accustomed to the baking heat at Beale in California, but the resident SR-71s of Det 4 at Mildenhall mean that the 'Q' is also at home in the lush Suffolk countryside

Tanker drivers don't often try 'mud moving', but
when they get a chance to put a big Boeing through
its paces, the sight and sound is impressive

Left In common with the KC-135, the EC-135 also has a tanker capability. The USAF's airborne nuclear command post can also receive fuel, as well as give it away. Boom out and receptacle doors are open for a low, slow flyby

Below Mildenhall is the home of four EC-135H airborne command posts, assigned to USCinCEUR and USAFE. One aircraft is usually deployed to Lajes in the Azores

Inset Under the shadows of Travis's control tower, a KC-135A basks in warm evening sunlight *(Courtesy Peter B Lewis)*

Main picture The 'E' and 'R' models may have more power, but there's nothing to compare with the fury of four J57s at full power. Four sooty trails are about to struggle into the evening sky at Castle AFB *(Courtesy René J Francillon)*

Top left The KC-135A (Boeing type number 717) was derived from the Boeing Model 367-80, the famous 'Dash 80' which first flew on 15 July 1954. The last KC-135A was delivered in 1966

Left The aircraft spotter's park at Mildenhall (kindly provided by the USAF), always gets a little excited when a KC-135Q screams over the fence. Where there's a 'Q', an SR-71 is likely to follow

Above Not so long ago, the grey Stratotankers weren't grey at all. In February of 1981, New Jersey Air National Guard KC-135As had grey engine cowlings, but silver prevailed (*Courtesy Peter B Lewis*)

Left A 42nd Bomb Wing KC-135A during a stopover at Goose Bay, en route to Loring AFB, Kansas. The KC-135A can carry 31,200 US gals of fuel in the wing and lower fuselage compartments (*Courtesy Fritz Becker*)

Above Tanker tails: a pair of Kansas ANG KC-135Es keep company with an RAF VC10 and TriStar, at Finningley, September 1987

Above The KC-10 Extender's bulky proportions often fill Mildenhall's hardstandings, but the attractive white paint scheme ain't gonna be around for long. Most KC-10s have received a particularly drab form of camouflage

Top right Sixty KC-10s will eventually be in regular USAF service. There's space for up to 75 personnel and 7567 cubic feet of cargo

Right The Boomer has a much more civilized environment in the Extender. His hi-tech equipment can deliver up to 1500 US gallons of fuel per minute (the KC-135 can manage 900), although this figure can only be gulped by the big stuff, like a B-52, as 1500 gallons per minute would blow fighters clean off the refuelling boom (*Courtesy Air Portraits*)

Victor

The Handley Page Victor is still in business. Last of the RAF's triad of V-bomber designs, the faithful Victor soldiers on. Inside the servicing hangar at Marham in Norfolk, this Victor has lost most of its flight instruments, as well as the main canopy. The long run-down to retirement has begun, and this aircraft was the first to be dismantled. The parts are placed in storage for possible use by the remaining airworthy aircraft in the fleet

Above Wearing the markings of the long-disbanded No 57 Sqn, this old lady also wears the grey/green disruptive camouflage which was standard to all Victors (and Vulcans) for many years

Right The glazed section in the nose was designed for visual bomb aiming, although it was rarely used during the Victor's career as a strategic bomber. In common with the Valiant and Vulcan, the Victor was equipped with H_2S bombing radar, operated by the nav-plotter in co-operation with the nav-radar in the rear-facing crew position. The visual bombing position did, however, become useful when Victors were employed on reconnaissance duties during the Falklands crisis

Left Vicious Victor. During 1986 one of Marham's tankers suffered a collapsed nose gear whilst landing at Ascension Island. The improvised patchwork covering the nose section got the Victor home safely, but the slightly mis-matched paintwork was the perfect excuse for a little artistic flair (*Courtesy RAF Marham*)

Above Graceful tails on the Marham flight line in 1986. Radar warning receiver (RWR) equipment is fitted to the tailfin bullet fairings

FUEL AS
PARENT
CAP 145 IMP. GALL.
646 LITRES

VALVE
X
2000 LBS/SQ. IN.
140·6 KG. MS/SQ. CM.

CONTACT LIGHT
RELAY BOX

Above left The Flight Refuelling FR.20B pod is fitted under both wings, and the pair can be operated simultaneously

Left On the ground, the hose basket is an untidy bundle of metal and canvas. Deployed in the air it's a beautiful sight, especially to a fuel-starved fighter jockey

Above Captain up the ladder first, and then the rest of the crew follow, ready for a three-hour fighter support mission over the North Sea

Overleaf, left Copilot's position, minus instruments and canopy. This tanker has flown its last mission, and awaits the attention of Marham's Victor dismantling team

Overleaf, right The rear crew don't have the luxury of ejection seats, although the pilot and copilot do. Originally the Victor was designed to have an escape capule for the whole crew, but design costs intervened. The nose section is, however, bolted to the main fuselage, along the original capsule separation line

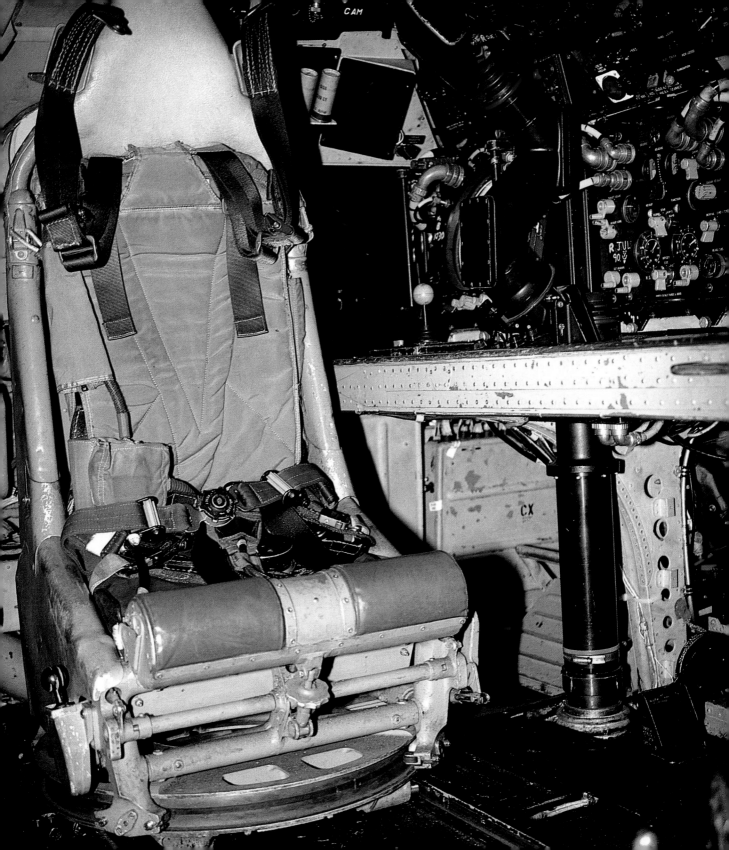

Main picture Lightning drivers would probably rate this as their favourite sight. The big underwing fuel tanks are fitted as standard on all Victor tankers, the smaller overwing fairings are aerodynamic modifications (*Courtesy Ian Black*)

Inset The author wanted to see how the Victor looked in the air, and No 5 Sqn offered me the 'flight of a lifetime' in a Lightning T.5. So, at 26,000 feet over the North Sea, Flight Lieutenant Mark Ims positioned us beside this combined Lightning and Tornado formation. Like every Lightning, the fuel flows away all too quickly in the T.5, and we quickly departed in search of a VC10 tanker, which was waiting for us

While a Tornado F.3 of No 29 Sqn blasts away in
the distance, the fighter pilot's friend rumbles along `
the taxi track, with the two fuselage-mounted ram
air turbine intakes open

Top Back on the ground (or nearly), an unmarked Victor K2 of No 55 Sqn touches down on Finningley's 200-ft wide runway, which was built to accommodate Vulcans

Above The last Victors aren't likely to leave Marham until the early 1990s, as the RAF intends to operate each aircraft until the very end of its fatigue life. The Falklands conflict demonstrated the Victor's versatility, when 13 tankers were scrambled from Ascension Island to refuel the Vulcan bomber which successfully cratered Port Stanley's Argentine-held runway

Against the sun, it's possible to picture these tankers when they formed part of Britain's nuclear deterrent, painted gloss white, and carrying a single Blue Steel stand-off nuclear bomb under the fuselage

Main picture Like the Victor and Valiant, the second of the three V-bomber designs also served the RAF as a tanker. During the Falklands conflict, the UK Ministry of Defence decided to convert six Vulcan bombers into single-point B.2(K) tankers. Two standard B.2 continuation trainers were retained in service, including XM597, a Falklands veteran. Under the nose of 597, the distant shapes of XH561, XH560 and XL445 sit on No 50 Sqn's dispersal at Waddington

Inset Many Vulcans were adorned with No 1 Group's panther emblem, especially during overseas deployments when crews from many squadrons utilized just a few aircraft. Rather than displaying the markings of individual squadrons, such Vulcans invariably acquired a Union Flag and a No 1 Group panther

Vulcan

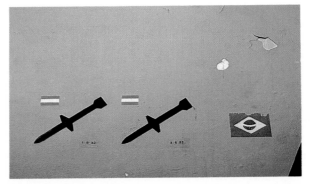

Above The markings on the nose of XM597 recall two anti-radar Shrike missions which were flown over the Falklands by this aircraft. One such flight nearly ended in disaster when a refuelling manoeuvre resulted in a snapped probe. The captain diverted to Rio de Janeiro, but arrived near the airfield at 20,000 feet (the most economical cruising altitude). The rapid descending turn which followed can't be found in any text book, but the crew landed safely with just 2000 lb of fuel—less than that required for a single airfield circuit

Above The only surviving Vulcan tanker is XH560, which is slowly decaying at Marham, still fitted with the hastily-applied HDU (Hose Drum Unit) and over-rotation warning sensor

Right The HDU was fitted in the Vulcan's ECM bay, so that an extra (third) fuel tank could be fitted in the bomb bay. Had it not been for the fact that the HDU's were needed for the new VC10 tankers, the Vulcans might well have still been in service today

Left Vulcan-to-Vulcan: the business end of XH561 doing its stuff high over the North Sea (*Courtesy Mike Jenvey*)

Above Vulcan B.2 XH558 appears at airshows throughout Britain. During 1988 the Vulcan Display Flight (an unofficial name, as no such unit actually exists), made a commemorative flypast over the Derwent Dams, where No 617
Sqn practised in their Lancaster B.1 (Specials) for the famous Dambusters raid of WW2. The Vulcan's crew comes from RAF Marham

Shortly before their retirement, No 50 Sqn flew a four-ship formation of Vulcans around Lincolnshire and the surrounding area, consisting of XL445, XH561, XH560 and B.2 XL426 leading (*Courtesy Mike Jenvey*)

Seen here refuelling a Phantom FGR.2, Vulcan
XH560 was converted to K.2 standard after serving
with No 27 Sqn at Scampton as a B.2 (MRR). After
taking part in the last Vulcan scramble on 14 March
1984, XH560 eventually flew to Marham (see page
70), where she still resides as a spares source for the
RAF's last airworthy example, XH558

Above The wrap-around camouflage of XH558 is representative of the low-level finish which was applied to a few airframes prior to their retirement. The high gloss finish is purely for protection and aesthetic appearance

Right The first and the last: not only is XH558 the RAF's last airworthy Vulcan B.2, it was also the first Vulcan B.2 to be delivered, on 1 July 1960

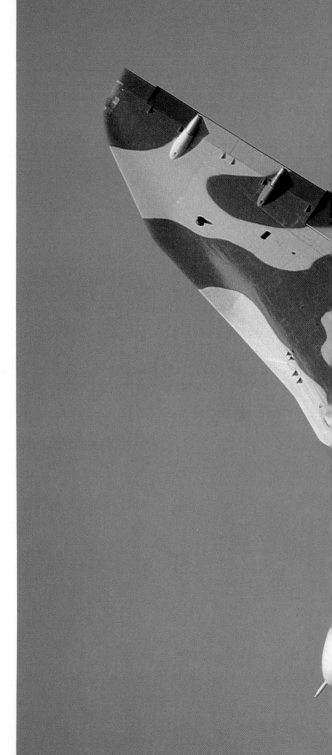

VC10

Left Much of the RAF's tanker support is now provided by a fleet of VC10 K.2s and K.3s operated by No 101 Sqn from Brize Norton in Oxfordshire

Above Looking upwards through a Buccaneer's canopy detonation cord, the majestic shape of a VC10 K.3 looms into view. The receiver in contact with the starboard drogue is another Buccaneer from No 208 Sqn, based at Lossiemouth in Scotland

Main picture Two tens are better than one: formating on a VC10 K.3 tanker of No 101 Sqn is a VC10 C.1 strategic transporter of No 10 Sqn, also from Brize Norton. The transports don't often fly with their bolt-on-probes fitted, as the VC10 possesses a very respectable range without AAR. As part of the ongoing crew training requirement, occasional sorties do include AAR practice. Two FAA Sea Harriers join in the fun

Inset The Royal Navy also likes to keep 'up to scratch' with their refulling techniques, and No 899 NAS kingly allowed me to chase a pair of No 800 NAS Sea Harriers from the back seat of a Harrier T.4N during March 1988

Main picture All of the RAF's VC10 tankers are pre-owned machines, having been operated as commercial airliners prior to conversion. The five K.2 'Standards' are all ex-British Airways, while the K.3 'Supers' came from East African Airways. The VC10 was a design masterpiece, albeit compromised somewhat in terms of cruise efficiency by BOAC's fatuous demand for a wing which would enable the aircraft to take off from the 'hot and high' airport at Nairobi at maximum gross weight. But it's a wonderful wing, even with pods slung underneath (*Courtesy Ian Black*)

Inset ZA149 'H' rumbles down Finningley's taxiway, accompanied by the distinctive whine of four mighty Rolls-Royce Conway turbofans. The RAF has 11 more VC10s in long term storage, awaiting possible conversion into tankers in the future

TriStar

Left It's huge and it's heavy. The RAF's biggest machine, the Lockheed TriStar

Above In company with a VC10 K.3 and its two Sea Harrier 'chicks', the TriStar heads eastwards over the Atlantic, bound for Brize Norton

In the wake of the Falklands crisis in 1982, the UK MoD decided that the RAF needed a significantly greater tanker capacity to make possible truly global or 'out-of-theatre' deployments by its tactical airpower. The fatigue damage endured by the already ageing Victor fleet meant that unless positive measures were taken, the RAF would be woefully short of tanker support by the early 1990s. British Airways had an over capacity problem at the time, and the RAF were able to obtain a fleet of six TriStar 500s from the flag carrier (and a further three from Pan Am) at a very competitive price. Snapped from the back seat of the aforementioned Harrier T.4N, these pictures feature one of No 216 Sqn's TriStars with its single point hose in trail. Eventually, the TriStars will receive wingpod-mounted HDUs, too

Above Finished in a pristine 'strategic transport' colour scheme, the TriStar is an impressive sight. Cleared for an all-up weight of 540,000 lb, it's a very capable machine. Despite the fact that the aircraft will be operated as a tanker, the majority of TriStar sorties are likely to be transport trips to and from RAF Mount Pleasant on the Falklands

Right Lining-up on Brize Norton's long runway, the TriStar's three Rolls-Royce RB.211 turbofans prepare to send the big L-1011 on a long journey south, to the Falkland Islands. Brize's runway has a long association with big machines; the Belfasts of No 53 Sqn were based here, as were USAF B-47s and B-52s

Falklands fallout. A great deal of rethinking took place within the Ministry of Defence following the Falklands conflict. The changes to Britain's defence policy and equipment were many, and the Vulcan tankers and TriStars were just two results. The Nimrod force also received plenty of attention, and the majority of the fleet were fitted with in-flight refuelling probes (taken from recently retired Vulcans). Re-designated as the Nimrod MR.2P, some aircraft also received Sidewinder missile fits. Who said the fighter jockeys have all the fun?

Buccaneer

Left Originally supplied to the RAF as an 'interim Canberra replacement', the Buccaneer was soon seen to be a world class strike aircraft; something the Royal Navy already knew. The first RAF Buccaneer squadron, No 12, was re-formed at Honington in October 1969, and now operates alongside No 208 Sqn at Lossiemouth in Scotland.

The RAF Buccaneer force still forms an important part of NATO's inventory, tasked with low-level maritime strike duties. As part of the Buccaneer's operational activities, aircraft are regularly fitted with wing-mounted refuelling pods, to act as 'buddy' tankers for other Buccaneers. **Above** From the back seat of a 208 Sqn Buccaneer, the classic shape of the Blackburn naval design towers overhead, as we take a drink from the starboard wing-mounted Mk 20C refuelling pod

Looking down from our fully-fuelled machine, two
208 Sqn machines demonstrate the art of buddy-
buddy tanking. In a wartime situation the RAF
tanker force would be in great demand. The tanker-
dedicated Buccaneer is a useful alternative

Above The 1988 Buccaneer display pilot, Flt Lt
Simon Smith, shows us how it's done. Nicely settled
in the basket, a look at the underwing stores reveals
an anti-radar Martel ASM

Top right Up into a lazy roll, and over we go.
Down below, our two playmates sweep across the
top of the Buccaneer's canopy

Bottom right The refuelling pod is always fitted to
the starboard wing, with a balancing fuel tank under
the port wing. Typical contact speed is 280 knots

Above The Boss (OC No 208 Sqn—Wg Cdr B Mahaffey) suggested we should take a look at the Buccaneer in it's natural element. So, down we go, and the cold North Sea starts to come up around the sides of the canopy—or so it seems. Our playmates break hard to port to practise a Pave Spike laser guided bomb attack profile

Left Thundering past the Orkneys cliff faces: the Buccaneer spends most of its time down 'on the deck'. It's fast and it's tough. And the ride is as smooth as glass

Above Back onto a long approach to Lossiemouth, the Buccaneer slows down to approach speed with the aid of the huge petal airbrakes. They're effective; 'like flying into a brick wall'

Top Out in the sunlight, the Buccaneer's naval origins are more clear; the wings fold, the nose and air brakes hinge inwards, and the landing gear was designed to take more punishment that you could ever give it. The bolt-on refuelling probe is permanently fitted

Left Buried inside its Hardened Aircraft Shelter, the Buccaneer sits ready to go. With four underwing-mounted Sea Eagle missiles, it's a force to be reckoned with. Would you fancy being on a *Kirov*-class battlecruiser when six Sea Eagle-laden bombers roar over the horizon?

The US Navy operates a large fleet of KA-6D
Intruder tankers. An F-14A Tomcat tops up as its
partner looks on (*Courtesy Stuart Black*)

Skywarrior

The ol' Whale is still around, albeit in steadily diminishing numbers. This KA-3B Skywarrior from VAK-308 is basking in Florida sunshine in October 1987 (*Courtesy René J Francillon*)

The USS *Kittyhawk,* March 1985, and another
KA-3B of VAK-308 is about to come aboard
(*Courtesy René J Francillon*)

This KA-3B entered US Navy service in July 1957.
Over thirty years later she serves with VAQ-34
(*Courtesy Fritz Becker*)

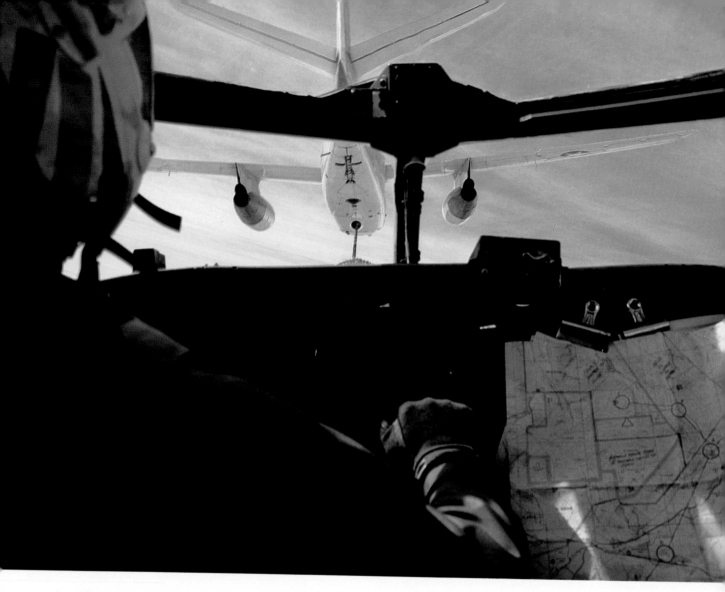

Above On the flight deck of KA-3B Bu No 147660: this aircraft was finally withdrawn in August 1983 after corrosion was discovered (*Courtesy René J Francillon*)

Right Low down, south of Barstow, California, (*Courtesy René J Francillon*)

Hercules

Left Up in the 'office' aboard a Lockheed Hercules C.1P, with a C.1K tanker sliding into view off the port wingtip. Another result of the 'Falklands Effect' is that the RAF currently operates a fleet of six dedicated Hercules tankers, split between RAF Lyneham in Wiltshire and the Falklands

Above At the rear of the flight deck, a scramble up onto the couch allows you to poke your head up into the astrodome. The view is superb, and if you've got the time, you can imagine yourself in the mid-upper turret of a wartime Lancaster, looking for marauding fighters. The fuel pipe, leading from the refuelling probe, runs along the top of the fuselage and disappears behind the wing trailing edge

113

Above The four Allison T56 turboprops keep churning away. You might spend the rest of the day on the ground, but your ears will still hear nothing but Hercules!

Right Out over the Atlantic, XV213 is waiting for us, hose trailing. The wingtip additions are electronic surveillance measures (ESM) pods

Overleaf, left Stabilizing behind the tanker before closing in on the basket. The fuel flow 'traffic lights' are clearly visible, as well as the yellow stripe running down the fuselage, used to aid the receiver in positioning behind the basket

Preceding page, top Up in the dome, the view of the refuelling operation is breathtaking. On a long training sortie the number of 'dry prods' seems endless, but the simple act of putting a probe in a basket ain't as easy as you might think. Every approach is just as exciting as the first

Preceding page, bottom Fuel flowing, and the two giants maintain contact in a gentle turn as we pass over North Cornwall. Down between the clouds, the ground crews at RAF St Mawgan in Cornwall can probably hear us, but they won't even bother to look up; we're in an Air Refuelling Area (ARA), and the distant hum of the Hercules is heard here every day

Above The HDU is fixed to the cargo ramp, and although the Hercules is de-pressurized while the hose is deployed, once it's aboard pressurization may be resumed

Two customers called in on their way to Norway,
resplendent in temporary snow camouflage. Two
Harrier GR.3s of No 1(F) Sqn, with bolt-on probes
at the ready

Above Looking through the captain's windscreen, the C.1P's probe points out to the distant tanker and its accompanying Harrier. The Hercules C.1K didn't enter service until August 1982, at which time the Falklands conflict had been settled. The long re-supply job had only just begun, however, and the Hercules undertook the bulk of this task. The captain of this C.1P, Flt Lt Terry Locke, flew one such sortie which lasted 28 hours, dropping spares to a Rapier missile battery at Port Stanley

Left The Hercules tanker is cleared to refuel every RAF aircraft which is equipped with a suitable probe. The list includes the Nimrod, Victor, Phantom, Tornado and others, as well as the Harrier

No Osprey Colour Series book is complete without
a look at the Lightning, and I make no apologies for
slipping in just one shot to illustrate the aircraft's
crude bolt-on probe. This basket's eye view was
taken from the rear cargo ramp of a Hercules C.1P.
Having flown me in a Lightning T.5 operational
trainer (XS458), Flt Lt Mark Ims brought F.6 XS923
up to the ramp for this oh-so-close study during
April 1988

Above If you're a really devoted Herky Bird fan, this house has got to be the place to live. Literally on the end of Lyneham's runway, there's an endless supply of RAF and overseas C-130s to admire

Right The tranquil beauty of a scenic corner of Wiltshire ain't so tranquil at all! Wait around for a while, and the air is filled by the buzz of four Allisons as another Herky Bird gets airborne

Above Positioned on a long final approach, in comes a C.1K tanker, back from the Falklands

Right Hercules XV188 is part of the LTW's fleet of 'probed' C.3s, and is therefore designated C.3P

Overleaf, top XV206—a C.1P, drifts in with the starboard outer prop feathered. Asymmetric approaches are a regular part of the Operational Conversion Unit (OCU) and Tanker Training Flight (TTF) courses

Overleaf, bottom Against a gloomy sky, a Hercules C.1P in the standard RAF tactical grey/green camouflage plus black codes and serials. It's a long way from the sand/stone scheme in which the aircraft was originally delivered. A rare overall pink machine was recently noted at Lyneham . . .